Winston Word Works -

The Usage Program

Teacher Manual

Copyright 1997

The contents of this book are fully protected
under the copyright and patent laws
of the United States.
No part of this book may be reproduced
without the express written
consent of the author.

Winston Word Works - The Usage Program

Precious Memories Educational Resources
18403 N.E. 111th Avenue
Battleground, WA 98604
Phone (360) 687-0282

Winston Word Works - The Usage Program

This course includes a unique selection of English usage challenges designed to eliminate over 60% of grammar errors occurring in everyday spoken and written language.

Students who master these principles will improve their grammar...to the surprise of all who listen to them or read their writing.

The practical and understandable lessons in Winston Word Works - The Usage Program were selected for their applicability to everyday language. Only those grammar constructions which cause common problems were included. We excluded grammar principles which, while valid in the detailed study of language, do not apply very often. We wanted to keep it simple and practical.

These techniques for grammar improvement were developed by the author of The Winston Grammar Program, a multi-sensory approach to understanding grammar, now delighting students and teachers nationwide. Winston Word Works is complementary to the basic course of the Winston Grammar Program.

A message to patrons from the author:

Trying to solve <u>all</u> usage problems, as most grammar programs do, is an overwhelming task. The effort fails because students get bored with the complicated rules and details.

We surveyed over 1450 English teachers at all grade levels and asked, "What <u>five</u> usage problems do you encounter most often and consider most important to solve?"

The results of that survey led us to include in Winston Word Works only those usage challenges deemed common enough and important enough to make a direct and positive impact on language skills. We estimate that the lessons in Winston Word Works tackle usage problems accounting for almost 60% of errors teachers find in student writing and speaking.

We hope you enjoy this practical approach to improving language skills.

Paul Erwin
Oak Island, NC
1997

Table of Contents

Student Worksheet #	Topic
Survey Test	To be taken before program begins (optional)
1	Review of subjects; action and linking verbs
2	Subject - verb agreement
3	Indefinite pronouns as subjects
4	Interrogatives; subject-verb agreement
5,6	Review and practice

Cumulative Quiz #1

7,8	Reviewing subjects, direct objects, predicate nominatives
9	Reviewing indirect objects
10-14	Personal pronoun case; "Divide and Conquer" rule
15	Personal pronouns as predicate nominatives
16	Mixed pronoun practice

Cumulative Quiz #2

17,18	Who and whom as interrogative pronouns
19,20	Locating clause boundaries
21,22	Who and whom as noun functions

Cumulative Quiz #3

23 - 27	Comparatives and superlatives

Cumulative Quiz #4

28	Sit and set
29,30	Good and well
31	Subjunctive mood
32	Less and fewer
33	Between and among
34	Three troublesome word pairs
35,36	As and than; Ellipses
37	Can and may
38	Bring and take
39,40	Lie and lay

Program Review A and B

Survey Test	To be taken after the program is completed

Directions for Worksheet 1

Students should review noun function cards one and two (red and blue). Worksheet 1 directs students to mark subjects with <u>S</u>; verbs should be double underlined.

After each sentence, students circle <u>A</u> or <u>L</u> to indicate whether the main verb is an action or a linking verb. Remind students that the most common <u>linking</u> verbs are listed on noun function card #2. If the main verb in the sentence is <u>not</u> on the blue card, it is an action verb.

Sample sentences for class presentation:

    He <u>bought</u> a set of laces for his skates.   (A)   L

    The old man <u>was</u> a miner during the 1930's.   A   (L)

Remind students that the <u>main</u> verb may follow one or more helping verbs. <u>Only the main verb matters when identifying action or linking characteristics.</u>

    We <u>have been</u> ill for a week.   A   (L)

    The gardener <u>has clipped</u> the hedge.   (A)   L

Proceed to Worksheet 1.

Directions for Worksheet 2

Subject-verb agreement with compound subjects can be confusing.

Many sentences have compound subjects linked by the coordinating conjunctions <u>and</u>, <u>or</u>, and <u>nor</u>.

        Bob and Mary <u>are</u> on the way to Houston. (s, s)

        Either the chairman or his assistant <u>has replied</u> to the letter. (s, s)

        Neither cars nor trucks <u>are allowed</u> on the field. (s, s)

(<u>Either</u> and <u>neither</u> are called correlative conjunctions when paired with <u>or</u> and <u>nor</u>.)

Useful rule - compound subjects linked by <u>and</u> take the verb appropriate for a plural subject.

        Several mice and a family of squirrels <u>invade</u> the cellar late in the fall. (**Not invades**)

        One fork and one spoon <u>are provided</u> with lunch. (**Not is provided**)

When compound subjects are linked by <u>or</u> or <u>nor</u>, the verb agrees with the <u>closer subject</u>.

        Either the captain or the recruits <u>are</u> in the barracks.

        Either the recruits or the captain <u>is</u> in the barracks.

        Neither the teachers nor the principal <u>agrees</u> with the policy.

        Neither the principal nor the teachers <u>agree</u> with the policy.

It is helpful to cover the first of the compound subjects with your finger in the four sentences above. When compound subjects are linked by <u>or</u> or <u>nor</u>, the correct form of the verb is easier to determine when you read only the <u>closer</u> subject.

Proceed to Worksheet 2

Directions for Worksheet 3

Some indefinite pronouns used as subjects cause stubborn grammatical problems.

> **WRONG** - Each of the accidents were reported.
>
> **CORRECT** - Each of the accidents <u>was</u> reported.
>
> > <u>Each</u> is a singular indefinite pronoun!
>
> **WRONG** - Either of the choices are acceptable.
>
> **CORRECT** - Either of the choices <u>is</u> acceptable.
>
> > <u>Either</u> is a singular indefinite pronoun! (So is <u>neither</u>)

There are many indefinite pronouns - <u>some</u>, <u>many</u>, <u>much</u>, <u>few</u>, etc. - but the three rascals above, <u>each</u>, <u>either</u>, and <u>neither</u>, seem to cause 99% of the problems. It is helpful to coach students to read the sentences adding the number <u>one</u> after the indefinite pronouns, <u>each</u>, <u>neither</u>, and <u>either</u>, and ignore the prepositional phrases between the subject and the verb.

> Each (one) ~~of us~~ <u>is</u> hungry and tired.
>
> Either (one) ~~of the chairs~~ <u>is</u> too small for her.
>
> Neither (one) ~~of the insects~~ <u>is</u> poisonous.

Proceed to Worksheet 3

Directions for Worksheet 4

Here, There, Where, How, When, What . . . Plus the Verb!

Sentences beginning with these words have subjects which appear <u>after</u> the verb!

    Where are my <u>socks</u>? My socks are where.

    How is your sick <u>aunt</u>? Your sick aunt is how.

    Here is your new <u>desk</u>. Your new desk is here.

Because of this subject-verb reversal, grammatical errors often occur if we are not careful.

Simply restate the sentence as above to see that <u>the subject must agree with the verb</u>. While the restated sentence may sound awkward, disregard that in favor of the proposition that we want to avoid poor constructions like:

There<u>'s</u> two reasons for my anger.	There <u>are</u> ….
Where <u>is</u> the salt and pepper?	Where <u>are</u> ….
When <u>is</u> the tryouts for the team?	When <u>are</u> ….
What <u>is</u> the farmer and his wife hoping for?	What <u>are</u> ….

Proceed to Worksheet 4, where students are required to complete the sentences by choosing the correct verbs.

    EXAMPLES:

Here's your choices for lunch.	Here <u>are</u> your choices for lunch.
Where is the people we expected?	Where <u>are</u> the people we expected?
There is three pens in his pocket.	There <u>are</u> three pens in his pocket.

Proceed to Worksheet 4

Directions for Worksheets 5 and 6

The next two worksheets offer students the opportunity to practice the subject-verb agreement principles learned in lessons 1 - 4.

Careful completion of these worksheets will prepare them for their first cumulative quiz, which follows worksheet 6.

Proceed to Worksheets 5 and 6

Directions for Worksheet 7

A thorough understanding of noun functions is absolutely essential to the correct use of personal pronouns and to the employment of other grammar principles. Worksheet 7 provides review and practice with subjects and verbs.

Students now use noun function cards (NFC) #1 and #2. Worksheet 7 should provide enough practice with subjects for students who have completed the Winston Grammar Program basic course. Additional review of subjects and all other noun functions can be effected by returning to Worksheets 21 - 27 in the basic course.

Using NFC #1 as a guide, students should easily identify the subjects in the following sample sentences for classroom presentation.

    S
I am a mechanic.

              S
During a crisis, you can count on her.

     S
Aren't they living in Denver any more?

      S
The plumber has arrived early.

          S
When are the apples harvested?

 S
Is Jason on board today?

Using NFC #1 and #2, students now identify subjects and determine verb types. The common linking verbs appear on NFC #2. There are some other linking verbs, but for the purpose of identifying noun functions, these are the only linking verbs to appear in Word Works. Assume that if a verb is not on NFC #2, it is an action verb.

Students first use NFC #1 to find the subject(s); they use NFC #2 to identify the main verb(s). Sample sentences for classroom discussion:

      S
The wind in the trees <u>is</u> delightful.   A (L)

 S
She <u>rode</u> a mare to the square dance.   (A) L

  S   **S**
Boris and I <u>can paint</u> the barn.   (A) L

          S
After her debut, she <u>became</u> quite a celebrity. A (L)

Proceed to Worksheet 7

Directions for Worksheet 8

The next worksheet provides review of subjects, action and linking verbs, direct objects, and predicate nominatives. NFC #3 (yellow) and #5 (green) are now available for student use.

Review NFC's #3 and #5 with students. Identify subjects, verb types, direct objects, and predicate nominatives. Sentences for classroom presentation:

       S
The rancher <u>sold</u> the (cattle).   (A) L

 S
He <u>will attend</u> (college) in the fall.   (A) L

   S   S   P.N.
Wyoming and Montana <u>are</u> mountainous states. A (L)

 S   P.N.
He <u>became</u> president at the age of forty.   A (L)

 S   S
I <u>married</u> (Sam) and we <u>have</u> two (children). (A) L ; (A) L

Using NFC's #1, 2, 3, and 5, students proceed to worksheet #8.

Directions for Worksheet 9

Perhaps the most difficult noun function to master is the indirect object. Only a small percentage of sentences in written English contain indirect objects. They are much more prevalent (and troublesome) in spoken language. When we proceed to compound pronoun usage, students will need to recognize indirect objects so that they can avoid such grating constructions as:

      Give Jim and I a chance to win.

      Mr. Parker lent Maria and I some money.

When we get to the "Divide and Conquer" procedure, we'll see just how <u>wrong</u> these constructions are.

Students review NFC #4 (orange). Sentences for classroom presentation:

      The mayor <u>gave</u> the [election] his best (efforts)   (A)   L

      Aunt Gladys <u>brought</u> [us] several (gifts)   (A)   L

Using NFC's #1 through #5, proceed to Worksheet 9.

Directions for Worksheets 10 and 11

The next two worksheets develop an understanding of personal pronoun case.

Students rarely use the incorrect form of a personal pronoun in a sentence where one pronoun is the subject of a sentence:

>Me want a puppy.

By the time most children are four years of age, they have self-corrected to:

>I want a puppy.

However, when personal pronouns are combined to form <u>compound</u> subjects, errors start to occur.

>s   s
>John and me went to the park.

This incorrect construction occurs because the <u>compound</u> subject makes the pronoun misuse less obvious.

Drill students in correct form by dividing the compound subject, reading each subject separately. This makes the correct choice of pronoun infinitely more obvious.

>s   s
>John and me went to the park.
>
>"John went to the park."
>"Me went to the park."

Students will reject <u>Me went to the park</u>; they will agree that <u>I went to the park</u> is correct.

Class practice with the <u>DIVIDE AND CONQUER</u> technique.

>s   s
>Betty and him carried groceries to the car.
>
>"<u>Betty</u> carried groceries."
>"<u>Him</u> carried groceries."
>— NO! —
>"<u>He</u> carried groceries."

Directions for Worksheets 10 and 11 (continued)

        s   s
The other men and us decided to leave.

"The other <u>men</u> decided to leave."
"<u>Us</u> decided to leave."
    — NO! —
"<u>We</u> decided to leave."

    s   s
Will you and him bring the lumber?

"Will <u>you</u> bring the lumber?"
"Will <u>him</u> bring the lumber?"
    — NO! —
"Will <u>he</u> bring the lumber?"

When students are ready to use the <u>Divide and Conquer Technique</u>, proceed to Worksheets 10 and 11, where they practice using the correct personal pronouns as subjects of sentences.

Directions for Worksheets 12 and 13

These worksheets require students to select correct personal pronouns for compound constructions following action verbs: direct and indirect objects. The "Divide and Conquer Rule" applies when forming these compounds.

Practice sentences for classroom use:

An ad agency hired she and I last week.

"The ad agency hired she."
— NO! —
"The ad agency hired her."

"The ad agency hired I."
— NO! —
"The ad agency hired me."

"The ad agency hired her and me last week."

The Senator gave her and I an award.

"The Senator gave her an award."

"The Senator gave I an award."
— NO! —
"The Senator gave me an award."

"The Senator gave her and me an award."

Proceed to Worksheets 12 and 13.

Directions for Worksheet 14

Personal pronouns used as compound objects of prepositions are often confusing. Like the compound constructions studied on Worksheets 10 - 13, the "Divide and Conquer Rule" applies.

Some sentences for classroom discussion:

>They left some apples for <u>you</u> and <u>I</u>.
>
>>"They left some apples for <u>you</u>."
>>"They left some apples for <u>I</u>."
>>— NO! —
>>"They left some apples for <u>me</u>."
>>"They left some apples for <u>you</u> and <u>me</u>."
>
>They developed the pictures of <u>you</u> and <u>they</u>.
>
>>"They developed the pictures of <u>you</u>."
>>"They developed the pictures of <u>they</u>."
>>— NO! —
>>"They developed the pictures of <u>them</u>."
>>"They developed the pictures of <u>you</u> and <u>them</u>."

Proceed to Worksheet 14.

Directions for Worksheet 15

Worksheet 15 takes up what may be the most difficult of the personal pronoun problems. Students have to internalize a special rule.

> When using a personal pronoun as a predicate nominative, use the form correct for the <u>subject</u> of a sentence.

      S   S
Were you and I the winners?
                  P.N. P.N.
The winners were you and I.

  S   S   P.N.
She and I were officers.
              P.N. P.N.
The officers were she and I.

The subjective forms of the personal pronouns are: <u>I</u>, <u>he</u>, <u>she</u>, <u>we</u>, and <u>they</u>. (We do not list <u>you</u> and <u>it</u> since they do not cause confusion.)

"Who just came to the door?"
  S   P.N.
It was he.

Students will resist this construction — a few giggles may erupt ... but it is correct. Realistically, this grammar principle may not enjoy wide practice, but it **is correct**, and we do encourage students to use subjective pronouns correctly.

Proceed to Worksheet 15.

Directions for Worksheet 16

Worksheet 16 provides mixed practice with all personal pronoun issues covered to date. Students complete this worksheet in preparation for the cumulative quiz which follows.

Up to this point, students have been allowed to refer to NFC #1 - 5. Teachers may suggest that students try Worksheet 16 without the NFC's. Whether students use the NFC's on Worksheet 16 and the Cumulative Quiz, is up to the teacher. Our experience has been that it is appropriate for students to be allowed to refer to the cues on the NFC's at all times if they need to.

Proceed to Worksheet 16 and schedule the Cumulative Quiz.

Directions for Worksheets 17 and 18

The correct selection of who and whom is difficult for even the better-than-average grammar student. It takes careful study to master this pair of troublesome pronouns.

The key to understanding who and whom lies in our mastery of noun functions — review Basic Grammar, worksheets 20 - 30.

Who and whom are used as either interrogative pronouns ...

        Who is your favorite player?

        Whom did you find in the closet?

... or relative pronouns ...

        I know who you are.

        He is the candidate whom we prefer.

We will tackle the differentiation of who and whom used as interrogative pronouns first.

> A useful rule: Rearrange questions as statements **before** you decide which interrogative pronouns to use

Who is the next customer?   The next customer is who? (P.N.)

Whom did the committee invite?   The committee did invite (whom?)

Once you can rearrange questions as statements, you can easily select the proper pronoun.

    A useful rule: If the interrogative pronoun is used as a subject or predicate nominative, use who; otherwise, use whom.

Who is the leader in this class?   (Whom) can we find for the job?

[Whom] did you give the diploma?   (Whom) are you punishing?

Proceed to Worksheets 17 and 18

Directions for Worksheets 19 and 20

Worksheet 19 requires students to locate clause boundaries. There are numerous rules that apply to this task which, we feel, make the process <u>more</u> difficult than the procedure outlined below.

For the most part, a sentence contains as many clauses as there are subject-verb combinations in the sentence.

      s   **s**
I <u>eat</u> whatever she <u>cooks</u>.

In the sentence above, there are <u>two</u> subject-verb combinations, so there are two clauses.

Students can readily find the clauses when asked, "Which two groups of words belong together?"

I eat . . . . . . whatever she cooks.

Try several sentences. First count the subject-verb combinations, then determine which words sound like they belong together.

    s   **s**
I <u>know</u> who you <u>are</u>.

I know . . . . . . who you are

     s   **s**
She <u>said</u> that you <u>could</u> <u>help</u> me.

She said . . . . . . that you could help me.

Try these:

You may choose whichever you like best.
                               Λ

May I have whatever I want?
                        Λ

Directions for Worksheets 19 and 20 (continued)

Sometimes the words that belong together are split in the sentence by another group that belongs together. Remember that each group must have a subject and a verb!

The sport that I like the best is basketball.

The sport <u>is</u> basketball ...... that I <u>like</u> the best.
      s   s

(This construction illustrates the use of an "embedded clause.")

We are <u>not</u> concerned at this point whether the groups of words (clauses) containing a subject and a verb are <u>independent</u> clauses or <u>dependent</u> clauses. Students are only identifying the boundaries of these groups.

Here are some additional sentences for classroom presentation. Brackets indicate clause boundaries for you. Practice these with students until they are ready for worksheets 19 and 20.

[I realize] [that I was wrong.]

[Can you hear] [what he is saying?]

[You may write] [whomever you wish.]

[The politician [I admire most] is not running.]
        (watch for the embedded clause!)

[That is the very point] [I made earlier.]

Proceed to Worksheets 19 and 20.

Directions for Worksheets 21 and 22

To determine the correct use of who and whom when they appear as relative pronouns, you must first isolate the clauses they introduce. Then you must determine each relative pronoun's use in its own clause.

> I know who you are.
> [who you are]
> *Inverted:* you are **who** P.N.

> William knew whom he would meet in Detroit
> [whom he would meet in Detroit]
> *Inverted:* he would meet **whom** in Detroit.

> A useful rule applies: If the relative pronoun is used as a subject or predicate nominative, use who; otherwise, use whom.

> We know who the boss is.
> [who the boss is]
> the boss is **who**   (predicate nominative)

> The pastor is a man whom we respect.
> [whom we respect]
> we respect **whom**   (direct object)

> Always avoid strangers who offer candy.
> [**who** offer candy]   (subject)

The same rule applies to the pronouns whoever and whomever.

> Please admit whoever arrives by 8:00 p.m.
> [**whoever** arrives by 8:00 p.m.]   (subject)

> You may select whomever you prefer.
> [you prefer **whomever**]   (direct object)

A cumulative quiz follows Worksheet 22, covering topics on Worksheets 17 - 22.

Proceed to Worksheets 21 and 22

Directions for Worksheets 23, 24, 25, 26

Worksheets 23 - 26 provide students with practice using comparative and superlative forms of adjectives correctly.

Adjectives form comparisons by changing to other words:

adjective	comparative	superlative
good	better	best
bad	worse	worst

by adding the suffixes er and est:

big	bigger	biggest
neat	neater	neatest

or, in the case of most longer words, by adding more, most, less, or least:

famous	more famous	most famous
suspicious	more suspicious	most suspicious
flexible	less flexible	least flexible

Use the comparative form when comparing two things; use the superlative when comparing three or more! Problems with these forms are generally limited to two specific confusions:

A) ...students rarely use the comparative form when required:

    He is the best of the two candidates. (better)

B) ...students incorrectly add the suffixes to words that don't take them:

    My dog is obedienter than your dog. (more obedient)

Worksheets 23 and 24 provide practice with the comparative and superlative adjective forms. Worksheets 25 and 26 require students to provide appropriate forms in sentences.

Proceed to Worksheets 23 through 26

Directions for Worksheet 27

Like adjectives, adverbs can be intensified to comparative and superlative forms. However, adverbs can only take <u>more</u>, <u>most</u>, <u>less</u>, and <u>least</u>; suffixes used with adjectives cannot be added to adverbs. The same rules apply: when comparing two attributes, use <u>more</u> and <u>less</u>; when comparing three or more, use <u>least</u> and <u>most</u>.

Sentences for classroom presentation:

    My dog eats <u>less</u> often than my cat.

    Of all my pets, my hamster eats <u>least</u> often.

    Of all my pets, my canary eats <u>most</u> often.

    The third candidate spoke <u>least</u> effectively.

    The second candidate spoke <u>less</u> effectively than the first.

A cumulative quiz follows Worksheet 27.

Proceed to Worksheet 27

Directions for Worksheet 28

The verbs <u>sit</u> and <u>set</u> cause unnecessary confusion. The distinction between them is easy, and a bit of practice will be effective.

<u>Sit</u> means <u>to occupy a seat</u>. <u>Set</u>, when used as a verb, means <u>to place</u>. The verb <u>set</u> almost always takes a direct object; <u>sit</u> almost never does.

You should <u>set</u> a lamp on the desk before you <u>sit</u> in the chair to study.

The principal parts of sit are: sit,   sat,   sat.

The principal parts of set are: set,   set,   set.

A few sentences for classroom practice:

<u>sit</u>, <u>sat</u>, or <u>set</u>?

Please _____ the glass on the counter. (set)

How long has he _____ there looking out the window? (sat)

She _____ the flowers on the hall table. (set)

_____ still while I cut your hair. (sit)

They _____ around the fire telling tall tales last night. (sat)

Proceed to Worksheet 28

Directions for Worksheets 29 and 30

Students often <u>incorrectly</u> use <u>good</u> in adverbial constructions:

    They play <u>good</u>.   The car runs <u>good</u>.

<u>Good</u> is usually an adjective: This is <u>good</u> pie.
    The debate was a <u>good</u> test of his speaking skills.

<u>Well</u> is usually an adverb: This house is constructed <u>well</u>.
    When I'm <u>well</u>, I'll resume my trip.

There are some adverbial uses for good (He is good-natured), and adjectival uses for well (The doctor doesn't often see well patients), but these constructions do not cause much difficulty.

First we look at the linking verbs associated with the senses: <u>feel</u>, <u>sound</u>, <u>look</u>, <u>smell</u>, and <u>taste</u>. These verbs often take predicate <u>adjectives</u>. When the choice of <u>well</u> or <u>good</u> is involved, choose <u>good</u>.

    Supper smells <u>good</u>.   That song sounds <u>good</u>.
    She looks <u>good</u> in red.   Asparagus doesn't taste <u>good</u> to me.

Confusion intrudes when we speak of <u>health</u>. <u>Well</u> is associated with how good our physical feelings are. I am <u>well</u> now. You don't look <u>well</u>. Was he <u>well</u> when he started the day?

<u>Smell</u>, <u>taste</u>, <u>look</u>, and <u>sound</u> are easier, but still cause problems.

    My bloodhound smells <u>good</u>.   My bloodhound smells <u>well</u>.

This pair of sentences illustrates the adjectival and adverbial distinctions which govern the use of <u>good</u> and <u>well</u>. In the first, perhaps the dog just took a bath. In the second, we speak of the extent to which his sense of smell is developed; <u>well</u> modifies <u>smell</u>.

Directions for Worksheets 29 and 30 (continued)

When you have a cold, you can't taste very well. (adv.)

This artichoke tastes good. (adj.)

She looks good.   She looks well.

Here we have the distinction regarding health. In the first sentence, we are commenting on the appearance she presents related, perhaps, to her dress, her age, her attractiveness. She looks well indicates our concern that she had been ill; her health is the issue.

Sound is rarely used with well, but it is correct to say, "He sounded well when I phoned him this morning." His healthy-sounding voice assured me of his well-being.

The most irritating of the good/well confusions come in more obviously incorrect constructions:

    He throws a knuckleball real good.

    You'll be healthy if you eat good.

    I couldn't write good after I sprained my wrist.

    I don't feel good if I eat too much.

Proceed to Worksheets 29 and 30

Directions for Worksheet 31

The subjunctive mood stubbornly holds on in our language and causes problems in everyday speech and writing. This remnant of older forms of language is still appropriate in today's grammar.

The words <u>if</u>, <u>wish</u>, and <u>as though</u> often trigger the use of subjunctive mood, where the verb <u>were</u>, usually associated with a plural subject, is used with a singular subject.

> I wish I <u>were</u> more energetic.
>
> If I <u>were</u> a poet, I would write sonnets.
>
> He acts as though he <u>were</u> an authority.

Students have certainly heard the subjunctive in use, and may have thought it was awkward. Many students resist using it for fear of seeming affectatious. However, the subjunctive mood still is the preferred form. We include an exercise to provide practice.

Proceed to Worksheet 31

Directions for Worksheet 32

Please indulge us.

Due to heavy misuse in television advertisements, most students cannot use <u>less</u> and <u>fewer</u> as adjectives correctly! Our survey results reflected widespread displeasure with this confusion. The author also finds the problem irritating. So, we include a lesson to erase these common blunders.

> **<u>Helpful Rule</u>**: If you can <u>count</u> the individual items referred to, use <u>fewer</u>.
>
> <u>Less</u> never modifies a plural noun!

I have <u>fewer</u> cavities than Fred. (Can cavities be counted?)

There are <u>fewer</u> lakes in Wisconsin than in Michigan.

Ice cream has <u>fewer</u> calories than fudge. (Can we count calories?)

Let's have <u>less</u> noise in the library, please.

We heard <u>fewer</u> noises as dawn approached.

Put <u>less</u> jelly in the sandwich this time.

Try a drill with students. Say the noun in the left column, then have students add <u>fewer</u> or <u>less</u>. Emphasis: can the objects be counted?

<u>teacher:</u>	<u>student:</u>	<u>teacher:</u>	<u>student:</u>
more copies	_____ copies	more chocolate	_____ chocolate
more fences	_____ fences	more fans	_____ fans
more trouble	_____ trouble	more bottles	_____ bottles
more links	_____ links	more candy	_____ candy
more clams	_____ clams	more candies	_____ candies
more pride	_____ pride	more boats	_____ boats

Proceed to Worksheet 32

Directions for Worksheet 33

For English teachers, here's a pet peeve! When we speak or write of something situated between or among other things, let's use the prepositions correctly!

When the object we speak of is positioned between two things, we've used the correct preposition. Otherwise, use among.

The circle is between two boxes.

The circle is among the boxes.

NO MATTER WHAT - BETWEEN MEANS IN THE MIDDLE OF TWO - AMONG MEANS IN THE MIDDLE OF THREE OR MORE.

The dots are among the boxes.

Each dot is between two boxes.

Proceed to Worksheet 33

Directions for Worksheet 34

Three troublesome word pairs appear often in student and adult language. They can easily be mastered.

beside - besides   farther - further   all ready - already

Beside is a preposition, meaning next to. Besides is usually an adverb, meaning in addition to.

> They slept beside the stream. Besides being avid campers, they enjoyed fishing. Besides, they would feel cooler near the water.

Farther is the comparative form of far ... far, farther, farthest. Farther and farthest deal with distance WHICH CAN BE MEASURED, in the sense of feet and inches.

> He can throw farther than anyone else on the team.

Further can be a verb meaning promote. (We will further the cause.) Further can be an adjective. (There was no further need for discussion.) Further also has an adverbial function often confused with farther, but the distance referred to cannot be measured in the sense of feet and inches. (We went no further into the investigation; the crime had been solved.)

All ready means all prepared. (We were all ready for the challenge ahead. The fish were all ready for the frying pan.) Already is an adverb meaning prior to a specific time. (The fish were already prepared for cooking.)

Proceed to Worksheet 34

Directions for Worksheets 35 and 36

The subordinating conjunctions <u>than</u> and <u>as</u> cause problems with personal pronouns. In both spoken and written English, they often introduce ellipsed clauses. Because the verb is missing from the clause, it can be difficult to discern that the <u>subjective</u> pronoun should be used.

       Tom is more aggressive than <u>me</u>.   <u>Wrong</u>
       Tom is more aggressive than <u>I</u>.   <u>Correct</u>

       Mrs. Porter is not as prompt as <u>him</u>.   <u>Wrong</u>
       Mrs. Porter is not as prompt as <u>he</u>.   <u>Correct</u>

These errors usually occur at the end of a sentence. If the ellipsis were more obvious, the correct pronoun would be used more often.

       Tom is more aggressive than I (am).

       Mrs. Porter is not as prompt as he (is).

By reminding students to <u>add the missing verb</u>, they will see the logic in this grammar principle.

Some sentences for classroom practice:

       I haven't been ill as often as <u>he, him</u> (has been).

       The other pupils finished faster than <u>me, I</u> (finished).

       My sister runs as fast as <u>me, I</u> (run).

       He received more votes than <u>her, she</u> (received).

       They are cycling faster than <u>us, we</u> (are cycling).

       There is no one more courteous than <u>us, we</u> (are).

       The guide was more cautious than <u>us, we</u> (were).

       Can't you type faster than <u>him, he</u> (can type)?

Proceed to Worksheets 35 and 36.

Directions for Worksheet 37

Teachers we surveyed complain that students use <u>can</u> and <u>may</u> incorrectly, and that the habit is difficult to break.

Actually, the distinction can be made clear very easily.

<u>May</u> is a helping verb. It is used to indicate <u>permission</u>.

> The officer says that we may leave.
>
> Mother, may I go to the pool?

<u>May</u> also shows <u>possibility</u>.

> It may be foggy, so be careful.
>
> That bear may attack at any moment.

<u>Can</u> is also a helping verb. It indicates the <u>ability</u> or <u>skill</u> to do something.

> Harry <u>can</u> fix anything around the home.
>
> I <u>can't</u> hear the train yet.

Worksheet 37 provides practice with this often confusing word pair.

First, some examples for classroom practice:

_____ we join you for dinner.	(may)
He _____ name all the states and capitals.	(can)
_____ elephants survive in cold climates?	(can)
You _____ enter if you give me a ticket.	(may)

Proceed to Worksheet 37

Directions for Worksheet 38

Bring and take are commonly confused verbs. They are opposites in their use when they mean "to carry."

To use these words correctly, a simple rule must be understood.

> Bring means to cause to come toward or with the person speaking or writing

John, bring your papers to me, please.
I will bring my lunch here tomorrow.
The puppy brings my slippers to me.

In these sentences, the speaker or writer is obvious, and an object is coming toward him/her or with him/her.

John, take your books to school, please.

We assume in this sentence that the speaker is not at school. This sentence indicates that someone is sending John off to school with his books.

John, bring your books to school, please.

In this sentence, bring is used correctly if the assumption is that someone at school is reminding John to have his books at school; this might be an admonishment from his teacher.

So, the student must determine who is speaking or writing and where the object is going -- toward the speaker (or writer) or away from the speaker (or writer).

There are certainly situations where the position of the writer is unknown, as in most narrative prose. In these cases, the distinction between bring and take is less important.

Harry took his clothes to the dry cleaner.

It is unlikely that the writer is at the dry cleaning store, so we chose took.

A. Sylvia brought her ticket with her.
B. Sylvia took her ticket with her.

In which sentence do we assume that the writer was at Sylvia's destination? (A.)

Directions for Worksheet 38 (continued)

I will <u>take</u> a snack to the game tonight.

In this sentence the speaker is carrying his snack with him, so <u>take</u> is correct.

<u>Take</u> these tools to the garage for me.

Here, the speaker is asking that the tools be taken away in the direction of the garage. <u>Take</u> is the correct verb.

Most errors using <u>bring</u> and <u>take</u> occur in <u>spoken</u> English, where the object and the speakers should be obvious. The sentences in Worksheet 38 are designed to make the bring/take issue easier to understand and apply.

Proceed to Worksheet 38

Directions for Worksheets 39 and 40

The most confusing of verb pairs is lie and lay.

Lie has two common meanings as verbs:
        to tell an untruth — Please don't lie to me.
        to recline or reside —   I want to lie down.
                                  Does the answer lie in your smile?

The principal parts of lie, meaning "to tell an untruth," are:
        I will lie;   Yesterday I lied;   I have lied.

The principal parts of lie, meaning "to recline or reside" are:
        I will lie;   Yesterday I lay;   I have lain.

Lay means to place or put:
        The army will lay down arms during the truce.
        Please lay flowers on the altar.

The confusions between lie and lay arise when we consider the principal points of each:

        I will lay;   Yesterday I laid;   I have laid.
        I will lie;   Yesterday I lay;   I have lain.

Notice that the past tense of lie is lay — confusing for sure.

Students should commit to memory the three principal parts of each verb. Class recitation and memorization shouldn't take long ...

        lie, lay, lain . . . lie, lay, lain, etc.
        lay, laid, laid . . . lay, laid, laid, etc.

Distinguishing the words at the meaning level will then guide them to correct usage. The major confusion comes with lay and lain forms of lie.

Directions for Worksheets 39 and 40 (continued)

Some sentences for class discussion.

I will _____ some bricks along the walk.	lay
Last week, I _____ some bricks along the walk.	laid
She retired to the porch and _____ on the sofa.	lay
I've _____ here for an hour, unable to sleep.	lain
Will you _____ beside the fire with me?	lie
During his trip to Moscow, the President _____ a wreath at the memorial.	laid
I had _____ there for several hours.	lain
I think I'll _____ on the floor and watch television.	lie
Please _____ the tablecloth and set the table.	lay
When we visited the hospital, we _____ our fears to rest... he looked great!	laid
We assumed the problem _____ with his poor study habits.	lay
The wounded man has _____ on the battlefield for two days.	lain

Proceed to Worksheets 39 and 40

Answer Key

Name _____

Date _____

Worksheet 1

Identify the subjects and verbs in the following sentences by making subjects with an S and double underlining all verbs. Circle A if the main verb is an action verb, or L if the main verb is a linking verb.

1. A gaily colored balloon^S <u>floated</u> toward the clouds.   (A)   L

2. He^S <u>read</u> the book over the weekend.   (A)   L

3. <u>Can</u> you^S <u>tell</u> me about the new neighbors?   (A)   L

4. The wedding^S <u>was</u> <u>scheduled</u> for June 17.   (A)   L

5. <u>Have</u> you^S not <u>been</u> <u>served</u> yet, sir?   (A)   L

6. I^S <u>changed</u> a dollar bill for four quarters.   (A)   L

7. James^S and Shelly^S <u>are</u> in Wichita.   A   (L)

8. The new kittens^S <u>will</u> <u>become</u> adult cats this winter.   A   (L)

9. The grass^S <u>hasn't</u> <u>been</u> <u>cut</u> for three weeks.   (A)   L

10. (You)^S <u>Turn</u> off the water in the garage.   (A)   L

Answer Keys

Worksheet 2

1. break
2. break
3. breaks
4. copy
5. copies
6. are
7. is
8. are
9. is
10. fly
11. fly
12. flies
13. fly
14. fly
15. flies

Worksheet 3

1. attacks
2. attacks
3. sees
4. sees
5. was
6. was
7. was
8. forgets
9. forgets

Worksheet 4

1. are
2. are
3. are
4. are
5. are
6. are
7. is
8. are
9. is
10. are

Worksheet 5

1. are
2. tells
3. mows
4. are
5. is
6. are
7. is
8. are
9. is
10. shade

Worksheet 6

1. is
2. are
3. drives
4. has
5. works
6. are
7. are
8. are
9. have
10. are

Name _____

Date _____

Cumulative Quiz #1

This quiz should be taken after completion of Worksheets 1 - 6.

In sentences 1 - 4, circle A if the main verb is an action verb; circle L if the main verb is a linking verb. Mark each subject with S.

1. The window above the stairs is dirty.   A (L)
   _S

2. We watched the variety show on Friday.   (A) L
   _S

3. The men of Rome and Carthage fought mightily. (A) L
   _S

4. One of the hamsters in the cage isn't mine.   A (L)
   _S

5. Either Tom or his brother is responsible.   A (L)
   _{S   S}

In the following sentences, write the correct form of the verb in the space provided.

1. Neither of the answers __**is**__ correct.   is,   are

2. There __**are**__ several jewels in the crown.   is,   are

3. Where __**are**__ my shoes and socks?   is,   are

4. Either my cats or my dog __**is**__ knocking these over. is,   are

5. Here __**are**__ some raisins for your lunch box.   is,   are

Answer Key

Name _____

Date _____

Worksheet 7

In sentences 1-5, find the subjects and mark them with an S. You may use Noun Function Card #1 (Red).

1.   ^SYou are an energetic employee.

2.   The ^Schimney was struck by lightning.

3.   ^SSnakes and ^Salligators are reptiles.

4.   Is ^SEaster in March or April?

5.   The ^Sconductor and the ^Sorganist were nervous.

In sentences 6 through 10, identify the subject(s) and verb(s) in each sentence. Determine whether the main verb is an action or linking verb: circle A or L accordingtly. You may use cards #1 and #2.

6.   The ^Shouse <u>seems</u> quite chilly today.   A (L)

7.   Several ^Sitems <u>were</u> <u>left</u> in the shopping cart.   (A) L

8.   The ^Steam of surgeons <u>saved</u> her life.   (A) L

9.   ^SClams and ^Soysters <u>are</u> <u>steamed</u> in salt water.   (A) L

10.   ^SI <u>became</u> upset when my ^Sfriend <u>was</u> <u>fired</u>.   A (L) ; (A) L

Answer Key

Name _____

Date _____

Worksheet 8

Using Noun Function Cards #1,2,3, and 5, identify subjects and verbs, circle A or L, circle direct objects, and write P.N. over predicate nominatives.

1. The porter <u>held</u> the two heavy (bags).   (A)   L
        [s over porter]

2. A tomato <u>is</u> actually a fruit.   A   (L)
        [s over tomato; P.N. over fruit]

3. The book <u>seems</u> long and boring.   A   (L)
        [s over book]

4. Smoke <u>can cause</u> lung (disease).   (A)   L
        [s over Smoke]

5. They <u>brought</u> the (criminal) to justice.   (A)   L
        [s over They]

6. Physics and Russian <u>are</u> very difficult subjects.   A   (L)
        [s over Physics, s over Russian; P.N. over subjects]

7. We <u>bought</u> (cups) and (saucers) at the antique store.   (A)   L
        [s over We]

8. Eerie sounds in the night <u>frighten</u> the bravest (campers).   (A)   L
        [s over sounds]

9. I <u>am</u> a poor speller but a good reader.   A   (L)
        [s over I; P.N. over speller; P.N. over reader]

10. The King of England <u>declared</u> (war) on France.   (A)   L
         [s over King]

Answer Key

Name _____

Date _____

Worksheet 9

Using NFC's #1 through #5, identify noun functions and verb types.

1. The teacher[s] handed [me] a (textbook.)   Ⓐ L

2. (You) Please read [me] a (passage) from the article.   Ⓐ L

3. The yellow ribbon[s] was tied to the oak tree.   Ⓐ L

4. Will you[s] bring [Bruce] and [me] a (sandwich) from the deli?   Ⓐ L

5. Can green apples[s] give [us] stomach (aches?)   Ⓐ L

6. You[s] must send the [buyer] a (deed) for the lot.   Ⓐ L

7. (You) Send [me] a (photograph) of your wedding.   Ⓐ L

8. We[s] watched several (shows) over the weekend.   Ⓐ L

9. Michael[s] saved [Jim] some (dessert) tonight.   Ⓐ L

10. The artist[s] drew [me] a (picture) of my daughter.   Ⓐ L

Answer Keys

Worksheet 10

1. she
2. They
3. he
4. we
5. we
6. I
7. she
8. he
9. I
10. they

Worksheet 11

1. I
2. she
3. he
4. she
5. I
6. she
7. he
8. I
9. we
10. she

Worksheet 12

1. me
2. him
3. us
4. him
5. us
6. us
7. me
8. me
9. me
10. us

Worksheet 13

1. her
2. me
3. me
4. him
5. us
6. him
7. us
8. us
9. me
10. her

Worksheet 14

1. me
2. me
3. us
4. me
5. me
6. her
7. me
8. me
9. me
10. me

Worksheet 15

1. she
2. he
3. I
4. he
5. they
6. he
7. she
8. she
9. he
10. they

Name _____

Date _____

Cumulative Quiz #2

Choose the correct personal pronoun for each blank.

1. The new waitress served my guest and ___**me**___. I,   me

2. It was not a fair trial for either them or ___**us**___. us, we

3. Inform my secretary and ___**me**___ when it is time for lunch. me, I

4. ___**He**___ and his dog take long walks each morning. him, he

5. Was it ___**they**___ who arrived last? them, they

6. It was the first opportunity for either Aaron or ___**me**___. me, I

7. Zach and ___**she**___ played checkers all night. her, she

8. The manager hired my cousin and ___**me**___ for the week. I, me

9. Will you or ___**he**___ be near the phone at 3:30? he, him

10. I predicted that it would be ___**they**___ at the door. them, they

Answer Keys to Student Worksheets

Worksheet 16

1. her
2. he
3. me
4. us
5. her
6. me
7. she
8. me
9. she
10. him

Worksheet 17

1. Who
2. Whom
3. Whom
4. Who
5. Who
6. whom
7. Who
8. whom
9. Who
10. Who

Worksheet 18

1. Who
2. whom
3. Who
4. whom
5. Who
6. Who
7. Whom
8. Who
9. whom
10. whom

Answer Key

Name _____

Date _____

Worksheet 19

Identify the subjects and verbs in each sentence. Then determine which groups of words "stock together." Put brackets around the groups to separate them.

Example: [I **respect** people]^s [who **tell** the truth.]^s

1. [She **knows**]^s [who you **are**.]^s

2. [I **think**]^s [she **has** a good idea.]^s

3. [The antique dealer **guarantees**]^s [whatever he **sells**.]^s

4. [She **remarked**]^s [that the temperature **had dropped**.]^s

5. [The editor **changes**]^s [whatever I **contribute**!]^s

6. [I **hope**]^s [you **will succeed**.]^s

7. [We **drifted** toward an island]^s [that **was** not on the map.]^s

8. (You) [**Take**]^s [whatever **appeals** to you.]^s

9. [I **drew**]^s [what I **saw**.]^s

10. [The rancher **retired**]^s [when he **sold** his livestock.]^s

Answer Key

Name _____

Date _____

Worksheet 20

Identify the subjects and verbs in each sentence. Then determine which groups of words "stock together." Put brackets around the groups to separate them.

1. [The book [I recently <u>read</u>] <u>was</u> biographical.]
   (s above "I", s above "book")

2. (You) [<u>Unlock</u> the door] [before you <u>enter</u>.]
   (s above "You", s above "you")

3. [The dishes [you <u>ordered</u>] <u>broke</u> during shipment.]
   (s above "dishes", s above "you")

4. [I <u>listen</u> only to music] [that <u>lifts</u> my spirits.]
   (s above "I", s above "that")

5. (You) [<u>Thank</u> the men] [who <u>fixed</u> the flat tire.]
   (s above "You", s above "who")

6. [The meal [we <u>ordered</u>] <u>was</u> too spicy to eat.]
   (s above "meal", s above "we")

7. [Because Bonnie <u>complained</u> so often], [we <u>ignored</u> her.]
   (s above "Bonnie", s above "we")

8. [Francine <u>was</u> the first person] [whom I <u>called</u>.]
   (s above "Francine", s above "I")

9. [A doctor [who <u>is</u> sick] <u>should</u>'nt <u>see</u> patients.]
   (s above "doctor", s above "who")

10. [If the tree <u>dies</u>], [it <u>may fall</u> on the house.]
    (s above "tree", s above "it")

Name _____

Date _____

Worksheet 21

Draw brackets only around the clauses which contain a blank where who or whom would fit. Determine which noun function who or whom performs in that clause. Use who for subjects and predicate nominatives. Use whom for all other functions. Indicate a noun function for who or whom in each sentence.

Examples: I wondered [*who* would make the speech.]
                              ˢ

   The painter [*whom* we most admire] is Picasso.

Who or Whom?

1. [The politician always knows [__(whom)__ he can influence.]

2. Can you tell me [__who__ that person was?]
                        P.N.

3. We cheered the man [__who__ saved the drowning child.]
                            ˢ

4. Hemingway is the author [__(whom)__ I read most often.]

5. The princess pined for the prince [__who__ never returned.]
                                          ˢ

6. That drill sergeant was a man [__who__ knew his recruits well.]
                                      ˢ

7. Can you find out [__who__ wrote this nasty letter?]
                        ˢ

8. We are gathered to honor a man [__(whom)__ we will all miss.]

9. [__(Whom)__ can we call] if we get lost?

10. If you find out [__who__ I am,] you will be surprised.
                        P.N.

Name _____

Date _____

Worksheet 22

Draw brackets only around the clauses which contain a blank where who or whom would fit. Determine what noun function who or whom performs in that clause. Use who for subjects and predicate nominatives. Use whom for all other functions. Indicate a noun function for who or whom in each sentence.

1. Did you wonder [**(whom)** I met today?]

2. We will applaud anyone [**who** (s) gets an "A".]

3. [**(Whom)** can we refer for this position?]

4. I felt sorry for the man [**who** (s) couldn't read.]

5. The guest [**who** (s) stayed too long] angered Mother.

6. Any employee [**(whom)** we find lazy] will be terminated.

7. Can you determine [**who** (s) has the fewest points?]

8. We arranged bail for the man [**(whom)** we considered innocent.]

In sentences 9 and 10, choose whoever or whomever.

9. You may accompany [**(whomever)** you wish] to the game.

10. I'd like to meet [**whoever** (s) planted this garden.]

Name _____

Date _____

Cumulative Quiz #3

Write the correct form in each blank.

who or whom?

1. To __whom__ was the package addressed?

2. We wondered __who__ the intruder might be.

3. The employee __whom__ we trusted most deceived us.

4. Is there anyone here __who__ can administer first aid?

5. Was it Bernard __whom__ we met in New Haven?

6. It was Truman __who__ said, "The buck stops here."

7. She never speaks to strangers __whom__ she meets on the bus.

8. __Whom__ did the critical article mention?

9. The Europeans __who__ immigrated became citizens.

10. I wonder __who__ left these tracks in the snow.

Name _____

Date _____

Worksheet 23

Write the correct form of the adjective in the blank. Use <u>more</u>, <u>less</u>, <u>most</u>, and <u>least</u> if required.

Adjective & Noun (comparing two)	Comparative Form (more than two)	Superlative Form
pretty blouse	prettier blouse	prettiest blouse
brave soldier	**braver soldier**	bravest soldier
* tasty recipe	tastier recipe	**tastiest recipe**
difficult problem	**more difficult problem**	most difficult problem
fair test	**fairer test**	fairest test
serious crime	less serious crime	**least serious crime**
* nasty cut	**nastier cut**	nastiest cut
successful attempt	less successful attempt	**least successful attempt**
adorable cat	**more adorable cat**	most adorable cat
healthy meal	**healthier meal**	healthiest meal
* fancy decorations	fancier decorations	**fanciest decorations**
thoughtful friend	more thoughtful friend	**most thoughtful friend**
important project	**less important project**	least important project
grateful guest	**more grateful guest**	most grateful guest

* be careful spelling these words

Name _____

Date _____

Worksheet 24

Write the correct form of the adjective in the blank. Use more, less, most, and least if indicated.

Adjective & Noun	Comparative (comparing two)	Superlative (more than two)
famous actor	**more famous actor**	most famous actor
desirable result	**more desirable result**	most desirable result
loud noise	louder noise	**loudest noise**
dry weather	drier weather	**driest weather**
small item	**smaller item**	smallest item
accurate shot	**more accurate shot**	most accurate shot
strange character	stranger character	**strangest character**
painful experience	less painful experience	**least painful experience**
witty speaker	**wittier speaker**	wittiest speaker
peaceful scene	more peaceful scene	**most peaceful scene**
smooth ride	**smoother ride**	smoothest ride
shameful act	more shameful act	**most shameful act**
crowded room	**less crowded room**	least crowded room
sharp point	sharper point	**sharpest point**
clear choice	**clearer choice**	clearest choice
quick decision	quicker decision	**quickest decision**

Answer Keys to Student Worksheets

Worksheet 25

1. stronger
2. smallest
3. fairer
4. wealthiest
5. older
6. younger
7. most dangerous
8. more fattening
9. farthest
10. better
11. worst
12. highest

Worksheet 26

1. smallest; best
2. larger; better
3. more colorful
4. more agile
5. more aggressive
6. longer
7. fewer
8. most talented
9. strongest
10. sunniest
11. larger
12. broader

Worksheet 27

1. less
2. less
3. least
4. less
5. least
6. most
7. more
8. more
9. most
10. more

Worksheet 28

1. sit
2. set
3. sit
4. sat
5. sit
6. set
7. sat
8. set
9. sat
10. sat

Worksheet 29

1. well
2. well
3. well
4. good
5. good
6. well
7. good
8. well
9. well;good
10. well;good

Worksheet 30

1. well
2. well
3. well
4. well
5. well
6. well
7. well
8. well
9. well
10. good

Name _____

Date _____

Cumulative Quiz #4

Write the correct word choice in each blank.

1. Of the two countries, Essex is the __**more**__ rural. more,   most

2. Moppit is the __**least**__ effective cleanser in the store. less,   least

3. His leg looks __**worse**__ than it did yesterday. worse,   worst

4. Which makes the __**better**__ punch, oranges or lemons? better,   best

5. Sheldon's first strategy of many was __**least**__ effective. less,   least

6. Of all his ailments, bursitis is the __**most**__ painful. more,   most

7. He is definitely the __**happier**__ of the two coaches. happier,   happiest

8. Mr. Franklin is the __**taller**__ of the two teachers. taller,   tallest

9. He had the __**saddest**__ expression of all the mourners. sadder,   saddest

10. We think Moses was the __**wisest**__ of the Prophets. wiser,   wisest

Answer Keys to Student Worksheets

Worksheet 31

1. was
2. were
3. were
4. were
5. were
6. was
7. were
8. were
9. were
10. were

Worksheet 32

1. less
2. fewer
3. less
4. Fewer
5. fewer
6. fewer
7. less
8. fewer
9. Fewer
10. fewer
11. less
12. fewer

Worksheet 33

1. between
2. among
3. among
4. among
5. Among
6. Between
7. among
8. Between
9. between
10. among
11. between
12. among

Worksheet 34

1. Besides
2. beside
3. beside
4. besides
5. further
6. farther
7. further
8. farther
9. already
10. all ready
11. all ready; already

Worksheet 35

1. she
2. we
3. she
4. he
5. we
6. he; I
7. I
8. she
9. she
10. I

Worksheet 36

1. I
2. we
3. he
4. we
5. she
6. he
7. she
8. I
9. I
10. he

Answer Keys to Student Worksheets

Worksheet 37

1. may
2. may
3. can
4. can
5. may
6. May
7. Can
8. may
9. can
10. can; may

Worksheet 38

1. Take
2. brought
3. bring
4. Take
5. take
6. took
7. take
8. Bring
9. take
10. take, bring

Worksheet 39

1. lay
2. laid
3. lie
4. lay
5. lain
6. lay
7. laid
8. lain
9. laid
10. lay

Worksheet 40

1. lain
2. laid
3. lain
4. Lie
5. lay

1. took
2. take
3. brought
4. brought
5. take

Name _____

Date _____

Program Review A

There is one usage error in each sentence. Cross out the offending word and replace it with the correct word.

Example: I wonder ~~who~~ she married.   *(whom)*

1. If I were you, I would try to contact your brother and ~~she~~. *(her)*

2. Brady, carry the food with you and share it with her and ~~I~~. *(me)*

3. She ~~laid~~ there for an hour, drifting further into her dreams. *(lay)*

4. The dogs found them and ~~I~~ among the bushes near the river. *(me)*

5. The bellhop told him and ~~I~~ where to get the key. *(me)*

6. Who has ~~less~~ parking violations? *(fewer)*

7. He went ~~farther~~ in the business world than she or I ever thought possible. *(further)*

8. We wondered ~~who~~ we could convince to drive us home. *(whom)*

9. Is he or ~~her~~ the wiser of the two judges? *(she)*

10. Don't lay your prints on his desk, ~~take~~ them to Bob and me. *(bring)*

11. Point to ~~whomever~~ raises his or her hand first. *(whoever)*

12. He has the better profile, but he gets ~~less~~ modeling jobs than I. *(fewer)*

Name _____

Date _____

Program Review B

There is one usage error in each sentence. Cross out the offending word and replace it with the correct word.

                                                    whom
Example: I wonder ~~who~~ she married.

1. We decided ~~who~~ [whom] we could ask to take on the responsibility.

2. Please ~~lay~~ [lie] here and wait for him or her to arrive.

3. They and we have ~~less~~ [fewer] arguments than we used to.

4. Can he or ~~her~~ [she] make the better fruit cake?

5. I've lain here much longer than ~~her~~ [she].

6. We couldn't remember whether they or we visited ~~most~~ [more] often.

7. Was it she who first mentioned my brother and ~~I~~ [me]?

8. She and I seek someone ~~whom~~ [who] can replace us some day.

9. Either of your plans ~~are~~ [is] bound to fail without our help.

10. I'll ~~take~~ [bring] the change back to him and her.

11. They laid ~~less~~ [fewer] cards on the table this time.

12. We should go ~~further~~ [farther] downstream before we lie down.

Name _____

Date _____

Usage -- Survey Test

Choose the correct pronoun from the choices to the right of each sentence.

1. The teacher and __**he**__ had a conference after school.   he,   him

2. Please give my brother and __**me**__ an opportunity.   I,   me

3. It wasn't __**she**__ who made the remark in question.   she,   her

4. Was it you or __**she**__ who made this quilt?   her,   she

5. __**Whom**__ did we finally decide to appoint?   who,   whom

6. Shouldn't you give the others and __**us**__ a second chance?   we,   us

7. If you and __**he**__ want help, just dial the phone.   him,   he

8. You and __**we**__ have little chance of success.   we,   us

9. __**Whom**__ can we call if we have a problem?   who,   whom

10. __**He**__ and his friends don't agree with us.   him,   he

Page One

Name _____

Date _____

Usage -- Survey Test

Each sentence may or may not contain a grammatical error. Circle the word used incorrectly if an error exists.

Example: Bob and (me) went fishing.

11. The inspector and I found her to be a prime suspect.

12. Will my client and I be able to see you and (he) before the trial?

13. Give my friend and (I) a better seat for the game.

14. Can you or she decide (who) you will nominate?

15. (Between) the three choices, she and I chose the first.

16. It was I whom she first spied in the crowd.

17. There will be (less) accidents if you and we drive carefully.

18. (Who) should we choose among all of the candidates?

19. She and I traveled the less bumpy of the two roads.

20. If he were a better hitter, he'd be in the starting line-up.

21. If you and he go (further) into the jungle, you'll get lost.

22. The other men and we decided to leave.

23. Adam developed the pictures of you and (they).

24. I wish I (was) more familiar with you and them.

25. Either the boss or one of his assistants is attending.

Name _____

Date _____

Usage -- Survey Test

Choose the correct verb form for each blank.

26. Either she or he ___**is**___ available to help.   are, is

27. Where ___**are**___ the blueprints for the project?   is, are

28. Neither of our choices ___**is**___ very appealing.   are, is

29. There ___**are**___ no good reasons for the delay.   is, are

30. Each of the officers ___**was**___ decorated for bravery.   was, were